The Changing Face of
MERSEYSIDE

The Changing Face of
MERSEYSIDE

Cliff Hayes

First published in Great Britain in 2002 by The Breedon Books Publishing Company Limited
Breedon House, 3 The Parker Centre, Derby, DE21 4SZ.

This paperback edition published in Great Britain in 2014 by DB Publishing,
an imprint of JMD Media Ltd

© CLIFF HAYES, 2002

All Rights Reserved. No part of this publication may be reproduced, stored in a retrieval system, or transmitted in any form, or by any means, electronic, mechanical, photocopying, recording or otherwise without the prior permission in writing of the copyright holders, nor be otherwise circulated in any form or binding or cover other than in which it is published and without a similar condition being imposed on the subsequent publisher.

This book has been written with all the lads who went to sea in mind. The ones who put their lives on the line in World Wars One and Two. The Merseyside men who kept England supplied with food and armaments, running the gauntlet crossing the Atlantic to keep the 'home fires burning' throughout those terrible war years. And the many thousands of unsung heroes, men and women, from Merseyside, who played their part in keeping Great Britain free.

ISBN 978-1-78091-449-7

Printed and bound in the UK by Copytech (UK) Ltd Peterborough

Contents

Introduction	7
Merseyside Before the Camera	8
Liverpool – the Heart of Merseyside	14
Going to Church	34
Liverpool's Outskirts	45
People and Places	58
Parks and Leisure	84
The Beat Goes On...	92
Full Steam Ahead	94
The Overhead Railway	101
A Life on the Ocean Waves	104
Birkenhead	115
Ellesmere Port	124
New Brighton	125
Port Sunlight	132
Wallasey	136
Southport	137
Widnes	148
Runcorn	156

Central Railway Station at Ranelagh Street, from an Edwardian postcard.

Acknowledgements

Thanks to Gordon Coltas (Locofotos) for his railway pictures. Thanks also to the team at Radio Merseyside for their continued interest in Liverpool people and their past. Thanks to Ted Gerry, postcard dealer from New Brighton, for his help, and to Jimmy of North West Books in Seel Street for some of the nostalgic ephemera I have used. Thanks also to Arthur and Eileen Haynes, postcard dealers, for searching out some of the rarer transport cards. And last but not least, to my wife, Sylvia, for her patience in putting up with me and the mess I make whilst creating my books, and for typing and correcting my work.

Introduction

MERSEYSIDE is a fascinating place. But what is Merseyside? It should be the land either side of the River Mersey, but the government decided to extend this area to include such unlikely guests as Southport, and so I dutifully include that resort in this book.

Of course, the city centre of Liverpool is well represented. And the outskirts too: Garston and its docks; Aintree and the Grand National; Speke and the airport; Waterloo and Walton; and Bootle and Sefton, the ones that got away.

It was always a pleasure to go to New Brighton, exciting and different. The open-air baths, the Tower, the funfair, New Brighton was a great place to be. Merseyside once had five open-air baths, but sadly they are now gone. It is this age of air-conditioning, we can't have a swim outside, even in the summer. I am not quite 60 years old, yet I can remember swimming and having a great time at New Brighton and Southport open-air baths. No doubt many readers will recall doing the same.

In *The Changing Face of Merseyside*, I have tried to show just that: how the area has changed over the years. I've tried to capture not only the buildings and the events, but also the people, in an attempt to capture the atmosphere of this great city and river over the past 100 years and more.

This book has been a journey through time and through the Merseyside area. I do hope you enjoy that journey.

Cliff Hayes 2002

Lime Street, Liverpool, and the Exchange Flags behind the Town Hall, about 1907.

Merseyside Before the Camera

THE Merseyside area is fortunate that many drawings of the Port, the Riverside and the many large houses, still survive, and enable us to get a better picture of what was going on during those formative years of Merseyside.

The word Mersey means boundary – it was the boundary between Lancashire and Cheshire – and up to a quarter of a century ago, Liverpool, West Derby, Southport etc, were all thought as being in Lancashire. The Wirral was considered as Cheshire. South Lancashire was a fertile area and attracted quite a few rich and influential families such as the Stanleys (Lord Derby), the Molineuxs (Lord Sefton) and the Norris family.

It is the paintings and drawings recording their lives and their properties which has added so much to our heritage and knowledge. Here is a small collection of some of those early drawings and maps.

A bird's-eye drawing of Liverpool taken from *The Illustrated London News*, 15 May 1886, showing 'all the new public buildings'.

Merseyside Before the Camera

A line drawing of the waterfront at Liverpool, from 1860.

An early Herdman drawing of the 'front' at Liverpool c.1860. It shows a landing stage. The structure on the right could be the pier which gave the name Pier Head to the area.

Speke Hall, the 15th-century home of the Norris family, as it was c.1850, after restoration by Richard Watt, a Liverpool merchant.

The interior of the hall at Speke in the middle of the 1830s, by G. & C. Pyne. Luckily, the hall has survived the ravages of the 20th century and is a lovely place to visit. Nestled away between the airport runway and the river, Speke Hall is a great source of Merseyside history. It is the ancient home of the Norris family and was acquired by Richard Watt, a wealthy West India merchant, in 1797. In 1942 it was taken on by the National Trust on account of the 17th-century furnishings introduced by the Watt family.

MERSEYSIDE BEFORE THE CAMERA

Hale Hall, in the quaint village of Hale, near Speke. The hall was built by the Blackburne family. Note the number of fake windows in the hall; window tax must have been in place at the time of this drawing.

A drawing from 1728 of Liverpool Tower. It was engraved by M. Gregson, for a book called *History of Liverpool* by Mr John Holt. In 1252, the Stanley family built a townhouse on the Liverpool shore. Henry IV, in 1404, gave Sir John Stanley permission to fortify and strengthen his home. But Sir John more or less pulled the old house down and used some of the stones to rebuild and fortify it as the tower, the building which we see here in this picture. It was used as a prison from c.1818 and included many French prisoners. It was pulled down after 1824 and a new white stone building was erected and finished in 1856 and called Tower Buildings, which is still there today.

The Changing Face of Merseyside

An engraving of Canning Dock and the Custom House from about 1840, by W. H. Bartlett. The Custom House was opened c.1835. The dock had formerly been a dry dock (Salthouse Dock) and was converted in 1823 to a half-tide dock of more than six acres. Canning Place was created on the site of Liverpool's very first dock, and second Custom House. Unfortunately, the beautiful Custom House in this picture was one of the many victims of German bombing during World War Two.

An engraving of Liverpool at the edge of the River Mersey, drawn by Samuel Austin c.1835. It is particularly interesting because it shows some of the shipbuilding yards. It also shows some of the tall smoking chimneys connected with manufacturing. The chimney in the far distance was that of the Herculaneum Pottery and was one of at least three large potteries in central Liverpool. The centre of the picture shows sailors in the ship's longboat, towing their sailing ship out to the Mersey Bar to catch the wind.

Another view of the town by Samuel Austin. St Nicholas's Church spire was completed in 1815. There had been a chapel here from Norman times. Liverpool was declared a parish in 1699. The white building on the right is a sea-water baths which stood where the Maritime Museum and Ferry Terminal are now.

Liverpool, the view from the River Mersey, about 1839. Even then Liverpool had a remarkable and recognisable skyline. George's Dock is on the left. It opened about 1788 after permission to build the dock had gone Parliament in 1761. Samuel Austin drew this picture, then the line drawing had to be engraved on a copper plate using wax and acid. This one was engraved by Robert Brandard.

The Changing Face of Merseyside

A close-up view of the area known as Mann Island, about 1840. Formerly known as Mersey Island, it was an artificial island created by the docks at the Pier Head. It was later named after John Mann, an oil-stone dealer who died in 1784. It ceased to be an island when George's Dock was filled. The white building on the left is the sea-water baths, which were a great attraction in Liverpool for many years.

Everton Village looks a charming rural village on the evidence of this drawing by W. G. Herdman, taken from an original oil painting of a view from around 1800. W. G. Herdman drew many views of Liverpool in the mid-Victorian period, but then turned his attention to oil paintings in art galleries and private collections and redrew many of them. Thus, it is not unusual to find Herdman drawings showing scenes from 50 or 60 years before he was born.

Everton Village grew up on a hill known as Sandstone Hill. From there could be viewed the growing Liverpool below. The Everton Cross had its top removed and made into a sun dial, as we see here. The double-roofed building on the left was the shop/house of Molly Bushell, who in 1759 made a confectionery and called it Everton Toffee. It was so popular that she turned her house into a shop and made many other types of sweets to sell to the public. In this illustration can be made out the tins and bottles etc in the windows. Several people tried to copy her recipes for toffee but never quite managed it.

One of the three low cottages was known as Prince Rupert's cottage and was his headquarters during the siege of Liverpool in the English Civil War. It is also said the Bonnie Prince Charlie stayed at this cottage and the chair he sat in is still in the hands of Molly Bushell's family.

Liverpool – the Heart of Merseyside

LIVERPOOL, the centre of the Merseyside area today, is about 900 years old, but West Derby is well over 1,300 years old and it was from here that area was once ruled. West Derby was the home of the Stanley family, and it was from here that they held court, issued the area's bylaws and collected taxes. It was 1,000 years before the roles were reversed and West Derby came under Liverpool's jurisdiction.

Like all good hearts, Liverpool has grown, taking in Everton, Kirkdale, part of West Derby and some of Toxteth Park in 1835. Sixty years later the rest of West Derby and Toxteth, along with Walton on the Hill and Wavertree, joined.

In 1902, Garston voted to join Liverpool and 1905 saw Fazakerley become part of the city. One thing that persuaded these townships to become part of the big city was the better facilities offered. Gas and water would be cheaper, rates were lower. In 1913, Allerton, Childwall, Little Woolton and Much Woolton also succumbed to temptation. West Derby Rural and Croxteth Park joined in 1928 and the last major change to Liverpool's boundary was in 1932, when Speke became part of the city.

A postcard showing five Liverpool features of 1928, at the end of which year it was sent as a greeting card for a 'happy new year in 1929'.

The Changing Face of Merseyside

Lime Street, Liverpool, a scene from probably late 1902. Lime Kiln Lane was cut in 1745 on the ridge where Prince Rupert put Liverpool under siege with his cannons in 1644. The name of the lane was eventually shortened to Lime Street in 1790. The large building dominating the right of the picture is the London North Western, built in French Renaissance style. The hotel opened in 1871 and was one of the largest in England. It has a frontage of 316ft and is five stories high, plus a basement. The Wellington Column is to the left. Note the very early open-topped electric tram passing the hotel. Today this fine edifice is student now accommodation for the John Moores' University.

Castle Street in 1903, with the Town Hall at the far end. Liverpool Castle was originally on the left-hand side of this view. When the castle was demolished, much of the stone was used elsewhere so there must be remains in the foundations of these buildings.

LIVERPOOL - THE HEART OF MERSEYSIDE

Castle Street and Liverpool Town Hall pictured in the 1930s.

Castle Street, Liverpool, c.1952.

Bold Street over a century ago, when the street was still cobbled. The street was named after the Bold family, and especially Peter Bold, a Liverpool merchant, who lived here.

A very early postcard view looking up Bold Street from Ranelagh Square. Bold Street was the 'posh' street with only the very best shops. The lady who wrote this card c.1903 commented: "What a lovely shopping street this is."

LIVERPOOL - THE HEART OF MERSEYSIDE

Lord Street, Liverpool, pictured from Derby Square, at the top of James Street. Lord Street was where the middle-class shopped, while Bold Street was for the rich upper classes.

A view from over a century ago captures a busy Lord Street with its open-topped horse-buses and passengers.

The Changing Face of Merseyside

Two views of Lord Street in the years before World War One. Open-topped trams pass each other under the ornate pole that held the electricity system.

LIVERPOOL - THE HEART OF MERSEYSIDE

Lord Street from a 1904 postcard. The young lad crossing the road on the left, the horse and groom centre, and the boy's face bottom right have all been added later.

Dale Street, Liverpool, from a 1905 postcard. Dale Street was the 'insurance street' of Liverpool with companies vying for the lucrative business of insuring shipping. They all wanted to show how 'solid' they were and built huge ornate offices in recognition of their importance.

St George's Hall, Liverpool. A postcard overprinted to be used as a Christmas card. The view does capture the length and size of the hall. Perhaps the designer, Harvey Longsdale Elmes, did not want this side to be admired as much as the entrance side. It certainly is just as imposing, but in a different way. The round end under the word 'Liverpool', houses a lovely theatre. Charles Dickens said that it was one of the best he had ever spoken in. There are also prison cells at this side at the bottom, although they are not clear here. The middle part of this frontage (which stands out) was a defence where police vans would drive in and close the two iron gates behind them before loading the prisoners for Kirkdale gaol. This stopped relatives, especially of those about to be hanged, from attempting a rescue.

LIVERPOOL - THE HEART OF MERSEYSIDE

A postcard from around 1907, of the Great Hall inside St George's Hall. The floor is one of its greatest works of art, made of encaustic tiles which cost £2,500 when bought in 1850. It does have a wooden covering used to protect the floor most of the time. The high ceiling is one continuous arch, 74ft wide, and the Great Hall is 169ft long. The organ at the far end reminds us that the original concept of St George's Hall was for it to be a concert hall.

A 1910 postcard showing William Brown Street, the Wellington Column and part of St George's Hall. Published by J. D. Grant, of the Arcade, Lord Street, Liverpool, it shows the view including Commutation Row, as it was just before World War One. Note how open and clutter-free the streets then were.

THE CHANGING FACE OF MERSEYSIDE

St George's Hall, Liverpool, pictured between the wars.

William Brown Street, on a postcard sent during World War One to a son away in the army – 'I have been looking in the papers every day for your name in the lost and wounded, and hoping not to find it.' The open-ended tram dates the view to about 1914. This street was formerly Shaw's Brow, but the area was levelled when St George's Hall was built, and the Corporation gave the land for public building. William Brown, alderman of Liverpool from 1831-38 and MP for South Lancashire, funded the building of a Free Public Library and Museum which were opened in 1860. The street was then renamed William Brown Street, and in 1863 William Brown was created a baronet.

Liverpool - The Heart of Merseyside

A closer view, again from a postcard, of William Brown's Free Public Library and Museum on the left. William Brown paid almost £30,000 for this building and also gave to other projects on Merseyside. On the right is the Picton Reading Room, erected in 1876 when the old Reading Room was proving too small. The £15,000 needed for this lovely round white-stone building was raised by public subscription and named after Sir James Allenson Picton, who was Chief Librarian at the time. In 1905, Hugh Frederick Hornby (he of Meccano and model railway fame) left to the city one of its greatest gifts, consisting of 8,000 fine art books, 7,880 antique prints, 3,000 autographs and other ephemera. He also left £10,000 to help house them and an annex was built on to the rear of the Picton Reading Room.

The next building up from the Picton Reading Room is the Walker Art Gallery, seen here on a 1914 postcard. A gift from Sir A. B. Walker, it was opened in 1877. Nine further rooms were added in 1884. The statues at the entrance are of Michelangelo and Raphael and in the murk on top is an allegorical statue of 'Liverpool', a female figure, wearing a castellated crown and laurel leaves. She is seated on a bale of cotton, a Liver Bird is beside her left arm. In her left hand she hold the propeller of a steamship, and a trident in her right hand, and at her feet there is a painter's palette, a compass and a set-square.

A 1924 postcard showing St John's Gardens (nicknamed Statue Park) and the row of fine buildings on William Brown Street. The tram stops at the bottom of the Gardens now have shelters. Just after this postcard was posted the whole area nearest the camera was dug up for the Mersey Tunnel (Queensway) entrance.

A picture of the same view as above but 10 years later. The tunnel entrance can be seen at the bottom of the picture, and it looks as though they are putting the finishing touches to it. The two bronze statues, centre front, are of King George V and Queen Mary. In 1994 they were removed and mounted on pedestals either side of the approach road into the tunnel.

LIVERPOOL - THE HEART OF MERSEYSIDE

St John's Gardens (the 'Stone Yard' some call it) is a lovely peaceful spot, pictured here c.1950, together with the Queensway Tunnel entrance. Two favourite statues in the park are those of Monsignor Nugent (1906) and Canon Major Lester (1907), both charity workers rather than statesmen.

Church Street, Liverpool, looking up from the Whitechapel corner, on a postcard from c.1904. The tall building on the left of the street is the Crompton Hotel. A middle-class travellers' hotel, it was popular with people waiting for boats.

THE CHANGING FACE OF MERSEYSIDE

Church Street, Liverpool, in the late 1950s. Bomb sites have been cleaned up into open spaces or rest and seating areas. The area to the left was the front of St Peter's Church which was once the Protestant cathedral.

Liverpool – The Heart of Merseyside

The Changing Face of Merseyside

A 1920s view of Church Street, Liverpool. The Crompton Hotel stands out as the tallest building on the street.

St Nicholas's Place, looking towards St Nicholas's Church, about 1910. The Overhead Railway runs across the picture. Far right is the Cunard Building under construction, the steel and re-enforced girders waiting to be covered in concrete. The white building next to it is the New Tower Buildings.

Liverpool - The Heart of Merseyside

Ranelagh Street, Liverpool, from a 1934 photograph. Crawford Cream Crackers, advertised on the tram, were made on Merseyside.

Ranelagh Street, Liverpool, and the entrance to Central Station, c.1910. The single-storey building on the right was the station buffet.

The Changing Face of Merseyside

This interesting postcard shows the Pier Head area before the Liver Buildings were built. It was posted in 1903 to Haslingden, Lancashire, and over the years made its way back to Liverpool.

The Pier Head in the 1950s, pictured from the air. From this angle it is evident that the Cunard Building is not square, being broader at the back than the front. It has nine offices at the back and seven at the front. The turning circles for the trams also show up prominently.

The offices of the Mersey Docks and Harbour Board at the Pier Head, seen here c.1910. There is no Cunard Building and work on the Liver Buildings would just have been starting.

The year is 1911 and now the Liver Buildings are on the left and Mersey Docks and Harbour Offices on the right. The Cunard Building has still to be built.

THE CHANGING FACE OF MERSEYSIDE

The Liver Buildings before World War One. There is a local joke that the Liver Birds are male and female: the female at the front is looking out for sailors; at the rear the male is looking for the football scores.

Liverpool - The Heart of Merseyside

The view from St John's Tower just after its construction in the 1970s. The Albert Dock is still be to redeveloped and Liverpool still shows the scars and open spaces left by heavy bombing during World War Two.

Going to Church

IN the 19th century, the upsurge of workers migrating into towns from the countryside made it necessary to build houses, shops and churches.

Churches for the Church of England were usually the first, then for Roman Catholics and Methodists, and churches and chapels for many other smaller denominations are all to be found in the Merseyside area. Today, however, in an increasingly secular society, many redundant church buildings are being either transformed for other purposes or demolished altogether.

Liverpool, of course, is renowned for its two cathedrals. They are both unique buildings and serve the people of Merseyside with pride and dignity.

In this chapter we take a look at some of the interesting church buildings of Merseyside, ponder at their existence or demise, and reflect upon the great acts of faith needed to construct many of them.

This is an artist's impression of how Liverpool's Anglican Cathedral would look when finished. But architect Giles Gilbert Scott altered his plans and the cathedral was never built like this. This 1906 postcard, published by Hugo Long & Co of Liverpool, and printed in Prussia, carried an appeal for funds to build the cathedral.

GOING TO CHURCH

Another artist's impression of the new Anglican Cathedral at Liverpool, built on land bought from the council and named St Michael's Mount. The smaller building on the left is the Lady Chapel, and was the first part completed, in 1904, and used as the church for many years.

The choir stalls and part of the Bishop's seat in Liverpool's Anglican Cathedral, taken from a postcard by Valentines from c.1930. Much of the red sandstone that was used to build the cathedral came from quarries in Walton and Runcorn. The Dean, Suffragan Bishops, and Canons all have their own seats here.

The Changing Face of Merseyside

The choir, looking east.

The Lady Chapel looking towards the organ, which was built by Jardin's. The Lady Chapel has beautiful windows featuring great women of the past.

The reredos from the north choir aisle.

View from the south-east transept.

St Luke's Church, Berry Street/ Leece Street, Liverpool. Most people refer to it as being at the 'top of Bold Street'. It was built in the 19th century to serve the middle classes who lived in the Rodney Street, Berry Street, and Hardman Street area. It was badly damaged during the blitz of May 1940, and the authorities decided not to rebuild it. It was left as a memorial to the people who lost their lives during the bombing of Merseyside in World War Two.

GOING TO CHURCH

One of the more unusual headstones to be found around Liverpool is this one in the graveyard of the 'Scotch' Church, Rodney Street. The gentleman buried here believed that pyramid shapes strengthened the brain and enhanced powers, and ordered that a pyramid be built over his grave.

Inside Sefton Church, c.1905. Note the pull-down chandelier lighting and the ornate rood screen.

The Changing Face of Merseyside

Top: St Paul's Church, Liverpool, from a 1908 postcard produced to raise funds. This card was sent from Liverpool to the vicar's daughter in Haslingden.
Bottom: A much older church in Huyton, pictured on a postcard dated 1912. Huyton, which came under West Derby, was a chapel of ease in mediaeval times.

Going to Church

If Huyton is 500 years old, Childwall is even older. Here are two views of Childwall Parish Church and Childwall Abbey. The Parish Church is dedicated to All Saints and has undergone quite a bit of rebuilding over the years. Childwall is an ancient area of Liverpool, its name supposedly deriving from a Saxon chief. After the Norman Conquest it was annexed to the barony of Manchester. Later, Childwall came into the possession of the Stanley family, then the Gascoyne family, then it passed into the hands of the Marquis of Salisbury. The district still retains an appearance of rusticity.

Inside St Catherine's Church, Edge Hill, c.1905.

The Roman Catholic Cathedral of Christ the King, Liverpool, the centre of one of the largest RC dioceses in England. It was begun in 1932 but a shortage of workmen during World War Two, as well as other factors, meant that the plans were altered and the Cathedral was not consecrated until 1967. Underneath the original vaulting, the crypt is absolutely beautiful, with wonderful brickwork.

Going to Church

This was St Peter's Church on Church Street, Liverpool, the centre of Anglican worship before the Cathedral was built in the early 1900s. The only sign that there was once a church here are two brass plaques and a cross in the pavement in Church Street. They are just to the camera's side of the post box

The Changing Face of Merseyside

Coincidentally, both Liverpool's great cathedrals have ended up very different from how they were originally planned. **Above** is a model of the original design for the Anglican Cathedral, by Sir Giles Gilbert Scott. It has two towers where today's cathedral has only one and is much smaller in the main body of the church. **Below** is Sir Frederick Gibberd's original plan for the Catholic Cathedral, based on St Peter's in Rome. It would have been the largest cathedral outside of Rome.

Liverpool's Outskirts

SOME 150 years ago, an unprecedented building boom took place in the towns of Merseyside, including Liverpool. Homes were needed for thousands of factory workers, and back-to-back houses were hastily erected. The more affluent white collar workers, who aspired to better things, moved away from the town centres to live in the fine Victorian villas that were springing up in the suburbs, their journeys to the office made easier by the developing railway system.

Heading north out of Liverpool city centre and up Scotland Road, in 1951. The road is a long, wide artery and a Parliamentary division of Liverpool. St Anthony's RC Church is on the right.

The Changing Face of Merseyside

Utting Avenue, showing the reserved running track for trams in the middle of the road so the vehicles did not get caught up in the rush hour.

A Liverpool Corporation tram heads up Warbreck Moor, Aintree, in the early 1920s. This is one of the roads that became packed with traffic when there were special events at Aintree Racecourse. Today, we associate Aintree only with horse racing, but at the time of this photograph there was also motor racing and occasionally motor bike racing and other events staged there.

LIVERPOOL'S OUTSKIRTS

Oakfield Road, one of the main roads in Anfield from late Victorian times. These large houses in this leafy road were in a very select suburb at the time.

Clifton Road, Anfield. Another row of grand houses. On the right are houses built with two-colour brick effect, popular from 1860 until the end of the 19th century.

The Changing Face of Merseyside

Monastery Road, near Anfield. A lone boy poses for the cameraman and someone has left their bicycle propped against the railings.

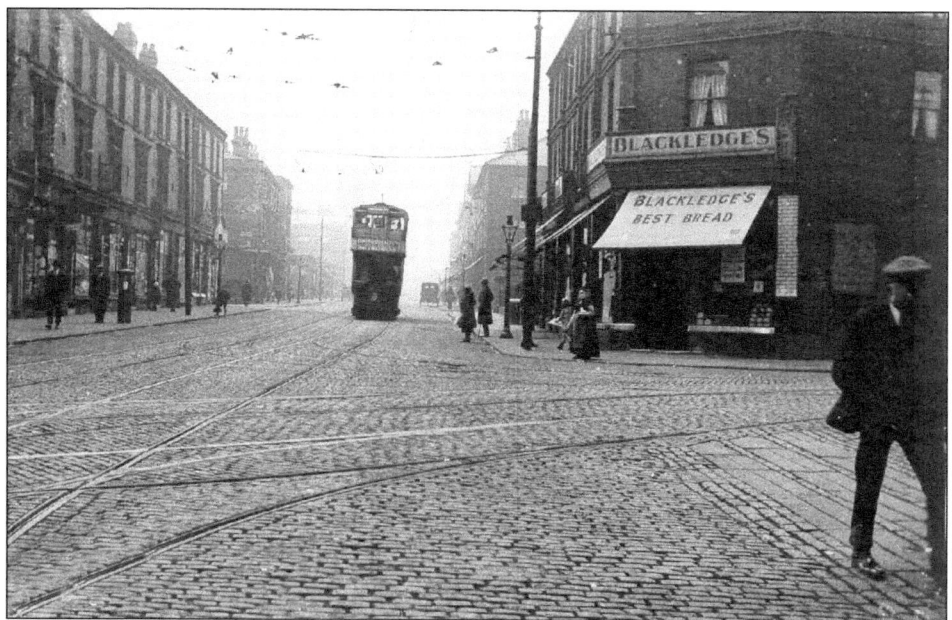

The corner of Breck Road and Oakfield Road going off to the right. Breck Road – the A580 – was one route to Manchester. Further up it becomes the East Lancs Road. Blackledge's Bakery can be seen on the corner, with plenty of other shops around it.

Liverpool's Outskirts

Clovelly Road, Anfield, about 100 years ago. These are typical of the top-of-the-range terraced houses built in mid-Victorian times. The bay windows gave a lot more light in the rooms of these tightly packed terraces.

Melling Road, Aintree, c.1900.

In the 1890s, Liverpudlians did not have to go far to find tree-lined roads, as this photograph of Orrell Lane, Aintree, shows.

Bridge Road, Blundellsands, Crosby, from a photograph taken around 1890. There is an area next to Blundellsands called Brighton-le-Sands, developed in Edwardian times.

Liverpool's Outskirts

Children playing on the beach at Blundellsands over a century ago. The large wooden structure on the beach was to show shipping the depth of the water and guide them in to the port of Liverpool.

Stanley Road, Bootle, at Strand Road corner, in 1906. Tram 68 has come from the Pier Head going north. Note Blackledge's delivery van on the far side of the road.

The Changing Face of Merseyside

Stanley Road, Bootle, early in the last century. Lord Derby, of the Stanley family, gave a lot of time and money to Bootle and there are many connections, including Stanley Gardens where there is a statue of King Edward VII unveiled in 1904. Derby Park was also a gift from the Earl of Derby, and although only 22 acres was laid out.

Bootle Town Hall, opened in 1882, and the Public Library and Museum added in 1887, as seen about 1933.

Liverpool's Outskirts

The Post Office and Municipal Buildings, Bootle, pictured in the early years of the last century.

The Technical School, Bootle, on a 1905 postcard.

King Edward VII statue in Stanley Gardens, given to Bootle by Lord Derby.

Testing the Burlington Street Bridge over the Leeds-Liverpool Canal on 4 June 1906, just before the bridge opened. The original terminus for the canal was Leeds Street nearby, but then traffic could go down to Stanley Docks and into the Liverpool dock system. There are plans to open all this again and across the Pier Head.

LIVERPOOL'S OUTSKIRTS

Burlington Street Bridge, over the Leeds-Liverpool Canal, pictured in the 1900s.

Blundellsands Road West, looking down to the 'beach' they planned there.

The Changing Face of Merseyside

The new three-storied balconied flats on Vescocks Street, off Blenheim Street, near Vauxhall Road, Everton, around 1920, the forerunner of the high-rise flats of the 1960s and 70s.

Liverpool's Outskirts

Tram No.970 heads up St Domingo's Road, Everton, on the 13A route (An 'A' meant the tram wasn't going the full No.13 route) in the early to mid 1950's. These round-ended trams were nicknamed 'pianos'.

An Edwardian view of Huyton, once an independent village miles from Liverpool. Now it is another suburb, although it did find fame in the 1960s when its MP was pipe-smoking, mac-wearing Harold Wilson, the Prime Minister from 1964-70 and 1974-6. This is Tarbock Road, leading even further out into the countryside at Tarbock.

Looking down Seaforth Road towards the docks in the early 1960s. Balfe Street is on the right. Wills's Woodbines, Oxydol, Capstan cigarettes, Tizer soft drinks and Lyon's Tea are all advertised on the corner shop which has two-colour bricks to show its 'superiority'.

The Changing Face of Merseyside

Delph Cottages, Knowsley, in the 1930s. Although now we refer to whole housing estates as being in Knowsley, originally it was just the village built by the Stanleys for their estate workers.

Liverpool Corporation tram No.951 climbs Brunswick Street and past the Corner House Café on the 29 route up to Everton and West Derby Road in 1953.

The end of the line for the tram at Knotty Ash terminal c.1910. Car 521 waits to begin its journey back to Liverpool.

Cowper Road, Old Swan, an Edwardian view of these typical middle-class terraces. Note that the road is just pressed earth and unadopted.

The Changing Face of Merseyside

The Sefton Arms, Aintree, from a 1912 postcard. Printers from Germany and Saxony would send out photographers to all major cities in Britain to take photographs of public houses, which they made into postcards to sell to the regulars.

A multi-view picture of Otterspool from the 1960s, although all four views are of the promenade. This was constructed with earth and clay taken from under the Mersey during the construction of the first Mersey Tunnel in the early 1930s.

Liverpool's Outskirts

A trolley bus (53) on the No.7 route to St Helens passes a tram on the 9A Prescot-Liverpool route just outside Prescot town centre in 1949.

This photograph was issued in 1987 as a postcard by the 'Get Prescot out of Knowsley" group.

Two young ladies pose with their bicycles at Sefton water pump in 1903. Sefton Well is behind them. The well was not the main source of water to Sefton although it had been for centuries before. Drinking fountains could be found all over Merseyside and were well used.

Balmoral Road, Elm Park, Newsham Park, c.1890. Alongside the park sprang up a development of middle to upper class houses. They were not as grand as those around Sefton but imposing in their own way.

King Edward VII, and later King George V made many private visits to their friend Lord Derby at Knowsley Hall. Sometimes the king would combine a private visit with a public duty, as happened in 1913, when locals and staff joined Boy Scouts a cadets to welcome George V to Rainhill.

Delivery boys pause for the cameraman in Portman Road, Wavertree, in the 1900s.

The Changing Face of Merseyside

Walmer Road, Waterloo, about 100 years ago.

The High Street at Woolton as it look just c.1895. Woolton was known for sheep and its by-products so it became the 'ton' (town) where wool was combed.

Liverpool's Outskirts

Marlfield Road, West Derby, in the early 1900s.

The road to Woolton, pictured in 1933.

People and Places

Selling fish on a street corner to make a few coppers. Liverpool women outside Great Charlotte Street fish market in 1895.

The unveiling ceremony of Liverpool's cenotaph by Edward George Villiers Stanley, 17th Earl of Derby. It took place on Armistice Day, Tuesday, 11 November 1930, before an estimated crowd of 80,000 people, at 11am immediately prior to the two minutes' silence. The veil was a vast green cloth to which 12,000 poppies had been hand sewn and which bore a Union flag and, in scarlet, the word 'Triumph'.

People and Places

Scenes early on 18 July 1934, when crowds began to gather to watch King George V and Queen Mary open the Queensway Mersey Tunnel.

The Changing Face of Merseyside

The King and Queen arrive with the Royal Standard flying.

The Royal car has arrived and troops line up waiting for the inspection to begin.

People and Places

This is how the Adelphi Hotel looked in 1914. It was called the Midland Adelphi then, owned by the Midland Railway Co, and rooms started at 14s 6d (73p) a night for bed and breakfast. In recent years the hotel has received a lot of publicity when television was allowed backstage for a series called *Hotel*.

Hartley's Village is off Lang Lane, next to the Aintree Industrial Estate. Wirral has Port Sunlight, built for soap workers, Aintree has Hartley's Village built by William P Hartley, for the workers in his jam, preserving and biscuit factories. People living in the area are used to telling people they live in Hartley Village (note most of them drop the 's'). Here we see the main street on a 1920s postcard.

Miss Janet Lamb, Bootle May Queen in 1913. May has always been the month for celebration in Liverpool and the May Day Horse Parade was the biggest in the country. May Queens from all the various areas would ride on dressed wagons in the parade, then have an official photograph taken.

Over 2,000 schoolchildren give a physical education display during the Liverpool Pageant of 1912.

People and Places

Two classes from Anfield Road Council School between the wars, possibly 1927. The photographs were found inside a copy of *Her Benny* at a book fair. The children pictured here would probably be in their 80s now. If any reader recognises a face here, the author would be delighted to hear from them.

The Changing Face of Merseyside

Strikes and strike-breaking has unfortunately always been part of the life of the docks on Merseyside. Here, police guard strike-breakers, during the 1911 troubles. It is not only Merseyside dockers who have used strike action to air their grievances; Liverpool, is one of the few places where the police themselves have gone on strike.

Shortage of manpower during World War Two led to the lowering of the minimum height for policemen. A whole division was recruited and called 'Bantam Police' after the small but fierce hen of the same name. Seen here from 1944 is the tallest and shortest policemen in the Liverpool force.

People and Places

Waterworth Brothers' Fruit Stores on Smithdown Road, Liverpool, c.1900. It must have taken an hour each day to lay out the fruit and vegetables, but pride in the shop made it all worth while. Photographers would persuade the staff of local shops to stand outside to have their picture taken, then would call back later and sell them the photograph as postcards at a cost for 12 of just two shillings (10p).

Another of those posed photographs, this time taken outside the Military Hair Cutting and Shaving Saloon in Richmond Row, with the barber and his assistant (probably the wife) caught in time c.1895.

The Changing Face of Merseyside

Children enjoy a paddle in College Road, Crosby, when it was flooded c.1960. A combination of high tides and heavy rainfall has often meant flooding in the Merseyside area.

There are worse places to be marooned than a pub. Flooding in Birkenhead in the early 1960s.

People and Places

Under the River Mersey in the new Queensway Tunnel in 1935. This is the Dock Branch at the Wirral side of the tunnel which allowed coaches to get to New Brighton and lorries to get to the Four Bridge area without clogging up the centre of Birkenhead. Queensway Tunnel was opened by a king and Kingsway Tunnel by a queen.

A rare photograph of the lifting section of the Overhead Railway. This ingenious piece of engineering enabled extra large or tall loads to get into the docks and away to the corners of the globe. After the load had passed, it would wind down again and the trains could carrying on running. (*See also page 101*).

The Changing Face of Merseyside

Upon the outbreak World War two the British Government ordered the closure of all cinemas, theatres and the cancellation of sporting events. Soon, however, it was realised that these were needed to help keep up morale. In this April 1940 photograph – a few weeks before the May blitz – a tram is running to the races at Aintree. Note the white-painted bumper to make it more visible in the blackout

Hoardings in Childwall Street, Kensington, Liverpool, in 1909. The Star Theatre is advertised as well as a boxing programme and the roller skating at the Tournament Hall, Edge Lane.

The neat and classy interior of Maison Lyons Café, on Church Street, Liverpool, about 1932. This was one of the places to 'be seen' between the wars. The photograph was taken by Stewart Bales of Union Court.

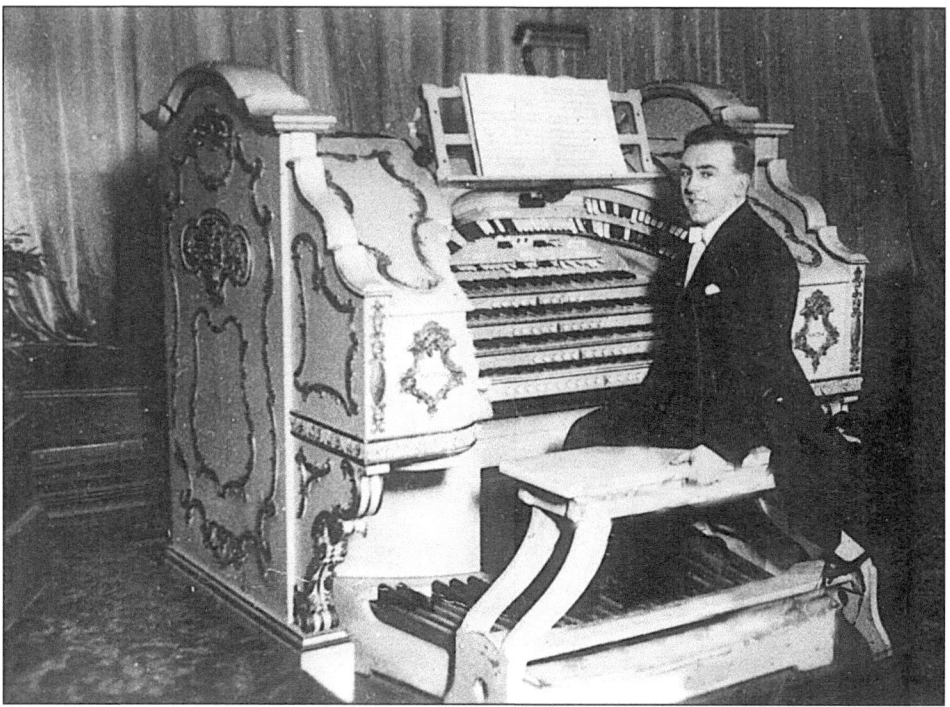

Rex O'Grady, organist at the Paramount Cinema, London Road, Liverpool, caught here on camera, complete with smile, in 1937.

The Garston Salvation Army band, pictured about 1937.

People and Places

The Grafton Rooms on West Derby Road pictured here c.1920. 'Olympia Twice Nightly' says the sign, but the Grafton has been everything for Merseysiders: a venue for works annual dances; films such as *Letters to Brezhnev* (1985) and *Dancing in the Dark* (1990) were filmed here; and Jeffery Archer once organised a student dance with the Beatles here.

A trio at New Brighton Baths entertaining the crowds before a beauty contest in the 1960s.

The Changing Face of Merseyside

Liverpool has some wonderful statues, and even today they keep springing surprises. This is the 'Banana Lamb' outside Lamb;'s, the ships chandlers, its third site in Liverpool. In the background is the Baltic Fleet public house, home of the Wapping Brewery.

A popular tourist attraction is this World War Two 'Duck', now painted yellow and renamed a 'Wacker Quacker'.

People and Places

Aintree is synonymous with the Grand National, and Red Rum perhaps the National's most famous entrant. His grave and his statue are fittingly contained within the world-famous course.

Passengers wait to board the *Royal Daffodil* ferry in summer 2001. The *Royal Daffodil* was built at Cammell Laird in 1962, and was originally named *Overchurch*, and first went on service between Woodside and the Pier Head terminal. She later underwent a major refit and assumed a famous local name. There had first been a *Royal Daffodil* in World War One, when the *Daffodil* was given its *Royal* title following its work at the naval engagement at Zeebrugge.

The Changing Face of Merseyside

The *Royal Daffodil* in mid-river, heading for Birkenhead in the late summer of 2000.

On Sundays the *Royal Daffodil* makes 'heritage cruises' and in this picture the ferry is heading downriver past the Docks in the summer of 2001.

People and Places

The world-famous view that welcomes visitors arriving at the Pier Head from the river.

The pre-war terminal of Liverpool Airport, Speke, is now a hotel.

Parks and Leisure

LIVERPOOL has more parks than other city in the North-West and these are the 'lungs' of this great city, providing green open spaces for its citizens.

Lord Derby and the Stanley family did much to provide these, and so too did the Sefton family.

Wirral is another green and pleasant area It has miles of scenic coast line with walks through country parks, and many leisure activities. Although it is across the water from Liverpool, it has a good public transport system, making it easily accessible, and is a favourite place for many Merseysiders.

The lake at Sefton Park, from a 1905 postcard.

Parks and Leisure

A 1906 view of Sefton Park Lake.

The Aviary and Bird House in Sefton Park, pictured in 1908.

THE CHANGING FACE OF MERSEYSIDE

Prince's Park, pictured here in 1907, is one of the smaller of Liverpool's Parks, but still full of charm and character.

This view from 1912 shows Prince's Park and the lake, together with the housing and flats which were so desirable, having been built on the edge of the park.

PARKS AND LEISURE

The Conservatory at Sefton Park.

The Palm House, Sefton Park.

Tam O'Shanter's statue, Botanic Gardens, Liverpool.

The Old English Garden, Greensham Park, Liverpool.

The Aviary, Newsham Park, Liverpool.

Parks and Leisure

King's Gardens, Bootle, 1907.

The Terrace at Liscard Park, pictured in the early years of the last century.

The Beat Goes On...

An advertisement reprinted from *Mersey Beat*, the first local music magazine and the first publication to feature the Beatles, the Searchers, Gerry Marsden and Billy Kramer. Here, though, Merseyside's rising stars play down the bill which was topped by American sensation, Little Richard.

The first anniversary edition of *Mersey Beat*, dated July 1962. Cliff Hayes started Billy Kramer's fan club and Cliff's 85-year-old grandmother was one of its first members. Billy used to stay at his house regularly and Cliff and would often drive the van for Beatles, Billy and the Coasters and others.

The Swinging Blue Jeans reached No. 1 in the charts in December 1963 with *Hippy Hippy Shake*. The day they reached this status they were booked to appear at the Locarno Ballroom, Liverpool, and (above) almost 4,000 teenagers turned up to see them.

THE BEATS GOES ON...

The Blue Jeans appeared on the popular BBC TV series *Z Cars* and sang three numbers. Here they are pictured with PC Jock Weir (Joe Brady) during the filming of the Christmas Day 1963 episode.

Johnny Sandon and the Remo Four were one of the classier groups around in the 1960s. Their act was polished and professional, but Pye Records did not have the clout enjoyed by Columbia and Decca. This is the group in August 1963, just after they had released a record called *Lies*.

The Changing Face of Merseyside

The Undertakers in a publicity photograph taken in Piccadilly, London, in 1964. From left to right are Brian Owen Jones, 'Bugs' Pemberton, Jackie Lomax, Chris John Huston and Geoffrey Nugent. When they started off the group used massive coffin-shaped speakers.

The Mojos were another of the groups to emerge in the Mersey Beat era. Here is a photograph of them at the *Top of the Pops* studio, Dickenson Road, Manchester in 1964. They were promoting their record *Seven Daffodils.*, which alas reached only number 30 in the charts. That September they were second on the bill on a Rolling Stones tour.

THE BEATS GOES ON...

A lady with a great voice, Beryl Marsden recorded on the Decca label and was perhaps unfortunate not to enjoy the same success as Cilla Black and Elkie Brookes.

Bottom left: Beatle mania – and there was a lot of it about at the time– sees fans sitting in Lime Street, Liverpool in 1963 reading the latest magazines about the group whilst waiting for them to appear.

Bottom right: The Beatle City Museum in Seel Street, Liverpool.

Full Steam Ahead

In ancient times Liverpool was a quiet backwater, ignored by the Romans. Wirral was just a woody headland with a small priory of monks. The Lancashire coast was, for the most part, undeveloped and the banks of the Mersey had only places of defence, Halton Castle being the most prominent of these. Then roads were slowly improved, and the late 1700s saw the arrival of the canal. The Shropshire Union at Ellesmere Port, the Weaver Navigation at Salt Port, and the Bridgewater at Runcorn. Goods started to be moved around the area, and industry and market gardening grew up on Merseyside.

The next important step was the railways; the world's first passenger railway was laid out between Liverpool and Manchester. The first scheduled passenger railway train left from Liverpool in September 1830. Liverpool was also the place where scheduled steam engines were still in use long after they had been abandoned in more southerly places.

The last scheduled steam-hauled British Rail passenger train leaves Lime Street Station for Preston with LMS 'Black Five' 45110 in charge on 11 August 1968. (*Locofotos*)

Full Steam Ahead

In 1930, a centenary exhibition for the Liverpool and Manchester Railway was staged. Engines were brought from all over England to Liverpool and the public were invited to inspect them and learn how they worked. Here we see '9599' being inspected at Wavertree in September 1930 (*Locofotos*)

Railway engines needed coaling and watering, and clinker and ash had to be dropped each night. This took place at what was was commonly called 'Sheds', but the official title was Motive Power Department. Here we see Brunswick Shed, which served Liverpool Central Station, with '7099' having just dropped her ash after a day's work. (*Locofotos*)

The Changing Face of Merseyside

Liverpool had many expresses coming from London and from 1920 onwards it became popular to give a name to a fast express that left at the same time each day. The train would carry a headboard with that name on it, and sometimes the coaches would have headboards with the name to help passengers get on the right train. *Manxman, Merseyside, Red Rose* and *Cunarder* were just some of these names. Here we see *Red Rose* in the 1930s with Royal Scot Class 46137 *The Prince of Wales's Volunteers (South Lancashire)*, nearing Liverpool. (*Locofotos*)

Southern Region engine *Lord Nelson* backs down on to a railway special at Lime Street Station in March 1981. For a time British Rail banned steam trains from the main line, especially under electric wires, so it was nice to see this one return.

Full Steam Ahead

For some reason LMS Black Fives were known as 'Mickeys' in the Merseyside area. Here we see Mickey 44764 with a heavy load of very mixed coaches nearing the end of its journey and approaching Edge Hill in the mid 1930s. (*Locofotos*)

It was one of those anomalies but Birkenhead came under the Great Western Region and trains from Woodside Birkenhead arrived in London at Paddington after a very circular journey including Chester and Shrewsbury. Here we see British Rail standard 92046, one of the most powerful freight engines, standing at Birkenhead Shed on 8 October 1967. (*Locofotos*)

The Changing Face of Merseyside

Rebuilt Patriot Class No.45527 Southport heads north on a London Euston-Liverpool Lime Street express in April 1953. (*Locofotos*)

Great Western tank engine 3627 waits with a full tender of coal, for its first duty out of Woodside Birkenhead Station in April 1930. (*Locofotos*)

The Overhead Railway

On 6 March 1893, a railway was opened on an elevated iron structure along the length of the Dock Road and was to become a feature of the city. It was the first open-air electric railway in Britain. The trains combined both traction and passenger carriage into the same self-contained unit. The 'Dockers' Umbrella' was a local institution but on Sunday, 30 December 1956, the last train rumbled over the line. Efforts to raise the £2 million for vital repairs were unsuccessful and demolition began in September 1957.

By January 1959, another chapter in Liverpool's history was closed.

A poster from the 1930s, advertising the Liverpool Overhead Railway.

The Changing Face of Merseyside

The bottom of James Street where the Overhead Railway crosses over to the Pier Head in 1955. The Overhead was still running and well used.

The Overhead Railway Station at the Pier Head, looking from the waterfront up Water Street. This really was a large station and the first public escalator in England was installed here.

The Overhead Railway

The Overhead Railway at Gladstone Dock Station c.1936. (*Jim Peden*)

Just once a year, the Overhead Railway was allowed to go on to British Rail tracks in order to carry extra people to the Grand National at Aintree. Here is an Overhead carriage at Aintree Station on 24 March 1956. (*A. C. Gilbert*).

A Life on the Ocean Waves

Life at sea was pleasant for the middle management and junior officers. This is the scene at a birthday dinner on the *Ocean Monarch* in the late 1960s, while crossing the Pacific Ocean. The author is on the far left with a junior deck officer, then Paul the barber, radio officer Sid, Glen the waiter, Paul the junior purser, and a junior engineer far right. I wonder what they are doing now?

Another birthday party on the *Ocean Monarch*, this time in the West Indies. Cliff Hayes is third from the right, back row. Next to him is John, night boss, from Formby. Hairdressers, stewardesses, pianist, junior officers and catering chief are also pictured.

A Life on the Ocean Waves

Chief Petty Officer Cliff Hayes, aged 22, the ship's printer.

The print shop on the *Ocean Monarch* and the author of this book in what was then his usual working gear – a small pair of shorts and a pint – together with his assistant, Norman. They were in Yokohama Harbour, Japan, for Expo 74.

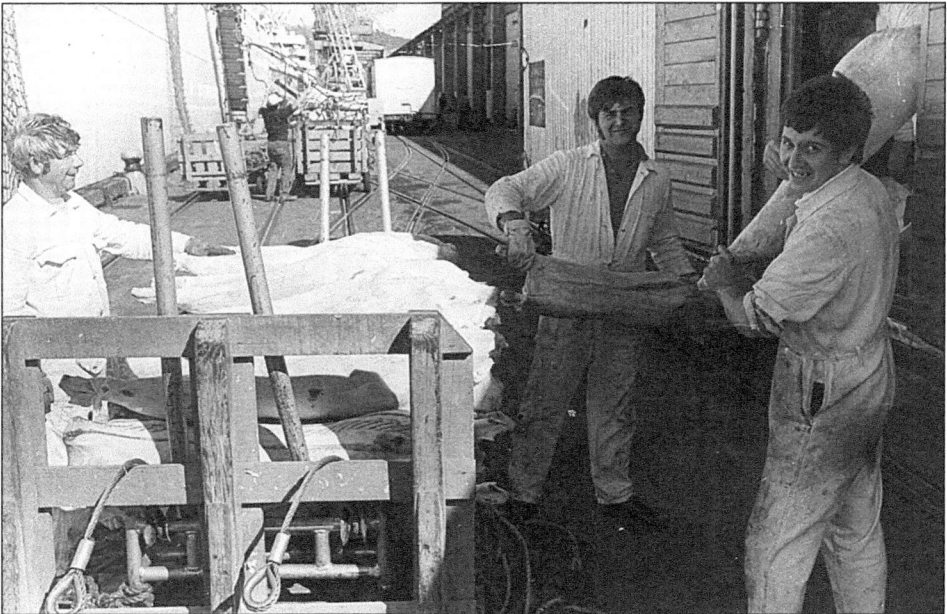

Life on a cruise liner was good, but there were also many cargo and passenger boats around and life on those could be much more interesting. The MV *Arawa* of Shaw Saville Line arrived in Wellington, New Zealand, to find a railway strike, so the ship had to go to Opua to pick up its cargo. Here three crew, the ship's joiner, the plumber (both from Merseyside) and author Cliff Hayes, earn some welcome 'cash in hand' overtime loading lamb.

Merseysiders took a pride in the ships in which they sailed and vessels out of Liverpool always seemed cleaner and better run than ones out of London or Southampton. Although there were always a good number of Scots and Irish, they blended in well and it was a 'Scouse' ship. This is the tourist lounge on the P & O liner *Stratheden*.

Many liners stayed in the river and unloaded and loaded. Others just came alongside the Pier Head to pick up passengers. In the middle of the river, of course, ships enjoyed greater security than if they were moored at the quayside. Canadian Pacific and Cunard liners went into dock only when they needed to their stores replenishing or if they were about to change from cruising to the North Atlantic run. This is Gladstone Dock in the mid-1950s, with a Manx boat and an Irish boat among others in the dock.

A Life on the Ocean Waves

A docker has his pass checked at the Gladstone Dock, Liverpool, c.1912. The ship in the dock is the *Lusitania*, built in 1907 and later sunk by a German U-boat off the coast of Ireland on 7 May 1915 with the loss of 1,198 lives.

Ships and shipping were part of everyday life on Merseyside. Here youngsters play cricket at Egremont in the summer of 1963 while the *Empress of Britain* slips downriver on her way to Montreal, Canada.

The Changing Face of Merseyside

A Cunard and a Canadian Pacific liner are caught on this aerial photograph of the docks at Bootle from around the 1950s. Note the lock to let ships out on to the river.

The Isle of Man Shipping Company vessel, the *Ben-my-Chree* ('Girl of My Heart') tied up at the Prince's landing stage just about to leave for Douglas, Isle of Man, in the summer of 1984.

A Life on the Ocean Waves

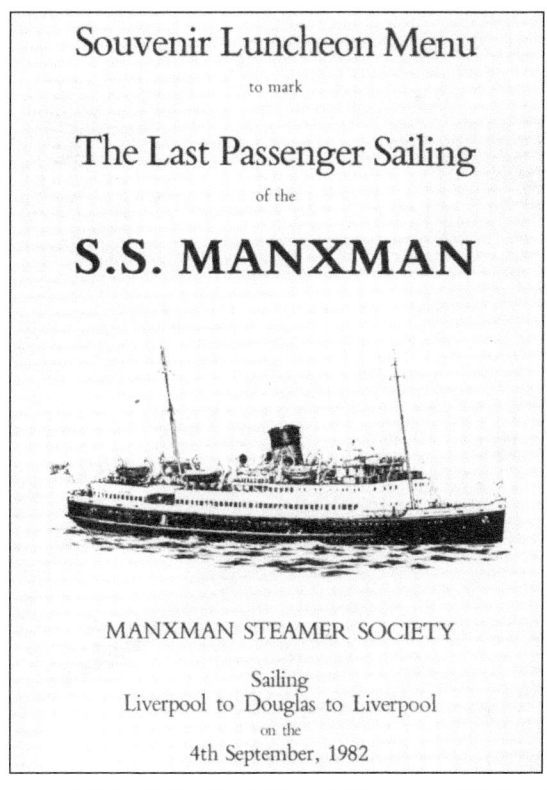

The Manx boats have always held a special place in Merseysiders' hearts, and people still sing about the *Ellen Vanin* which sank at the Mersey Bar. Here is the front cover of the menu for the farewell trip of the SS *Manxman* on 4 September 1982.

HMS *Britannia* heads up the River Mersey out to sea after a Royal Naval visit to Liverpool in 1904. New Brighton's distinctive tower still dominates in the background.

The Changing Face of Merseyside

Many of the great liners of the British merchant fleet were Liverpool-registered and well over 50 per cent of the crews on these liners were from Merseyside, even after Cunard and White Star moved to Southampton. Here we see the *Queen Mary* docking at Southampton in the mid-1950s. No doubt many of the crew were ready to head home to Merseyside.

A Life on the Ocean Waves

The landing stage at Liverpool on a Sunday morning sometime in the 1930s. The nearest boat is from the North Wales Steam Ship Company and will no doubt be leaving shortly for Llandudno and Bangor.

The *Empress of England* pictured on a postcard issued by the Canadian Pacific Company just after the ship had been repainted in the new company funnel logo and colours. This ship later became the *Ocean Monarch*.

The Changing Face of Merseyside

Wapping Goods Warehouse on the docks at Liverpool in May 1962. The docks could be dismal places with lots of bays, back alleyways and corners, but fascinating to look back at.

The *Saxonia* of the Cunard Line at Liverpool assisted by tugs around 1925. At the time there was up to 25 tugs working on the river.

A well-worn coastal vessel slips into the Manchester Ship Canal at Eastham with a cargo of wooden railway sleepers c.1910.

HMS *Invincible* caught in stark silhouette on her visit to the River Mersey in the summer of 2001.

The Changing Face of Merseyside

The Royal Yacht *Britannia* in the River Mersey being towed alongside the landing stage on 20 June 1977.

Today when any special visiting ships arrive in the River Mersey, ferries are always available to take people to have a closer look at them. This happened when HMS *Invincible*, seen here in June 2000, anchored in the river for a five-day visit.

The Isle of Man Steamship Co's *Lady of Man* waits at the Pier Head before its return journey to Douglas in summer 2000.

Birkenhead

Birkenhead owes its origins to the monks of Chester Monastery, who set up a priory here c.1150. From here they ferried people across the river to continue their journey south. The crossing became known as Monks' Ferry, then later as Woodside Ferry. This is the approach to the ferry pictured in 1904.

By the end of the 18th century, Birkenhead could not even be called a village and then the effects of the Industrial Revolution turned it into a thriving town. This is Birkenhead Market Place on a Saturday night c.1902, when hundreds of people came looking for late bargain.

The Changing Face of Merseyside

Merseyside has long enjoyed an integrated transport system. Here, trams and buses at Woodside Ferry wait for the homeward rush of people off the ferry, c.1930.

A restored Victorian horse-drawn tram at the Ferry Terminal, Birkenhead, in 1996. Birkenhead was the first place in Great Britain to have what was called a 'street railway'. In August 1860 a service started from the ferry terminal at Woodside to Birkenhead Park. The tramway became electrified and taken over by the Corporation in 1901. Birkenhead trams ran until 17 July 1937.

This tram was rescued from being a hen house in Formby, and restored by the Merseyside Tram Preservation Society. The society also runs trams, original and rebuilt, from outside the Woodside Ferry to their museum and headquarters just off Pacific Road.

Birkenhead

Borough Road, Birkenhead c.1909. It was laid out when Birkenhead became a borough in 1877.

Argyle Street, Birkenhead, said to be named after the birthplace of John Laird's mother in Scotland. The Argyle Theatre can be seen to the left and it was from here that some early radio programmes were broadcast. This picture is from c.1904.

The Changing Face of Merseyside

Argyle Street, Birkenhead, c.1904. The open-topped tram was one of the first to be powered by electricity in Birkenhead. The town's popular billiard hall is on the right.

Conway Street, Birkenhead, as it looked c.1907. The tram service which ran from Woodside Ferry began in August 1860.

BIRKENHEAD

A busy shopping day on Grange Road in November 1956. Today, pedestrianised, it is the heart of Birkenhead's shopping area.

The Changing Face of Merseyside

Hamilton Square, Birkenhead, c.1920. The square was laid out by William Laird, with the formal gridiron pattern of long straight roads radiating from it. The gardens were once private and fenced-off, and each resident had their own key, so that the general public were kept out.

Hamilton Square pictured over 40 years later. The private homes have now all gone and prestigious offices now occupy the grand houses. The year is 1965 and the Corporation bus is starting the 86 South Circle route via Bromborough Road.

BIRKENHEAD

The blitz on Liverpool during World War Two is well-documented, but the Wirral, particularly Birkenhead and Wallasey, also took awful poundings. The docks at Four Bridges, Birkenhead, was a prime target because it was here that vital supplies from the USA and Canada were unloaded. The heaviest raids took place on 12-13 March 1941, when 288 people were killed. This picture shows three residents defiantly flying the Union flag amidst the rubble of their homes.

St Mary's Church, Birkenhead, pictured in 2001. The main body of the church has now been demolished, but the clock tower and spire still remain. This church was once the parish church of Birkenhead, but when the tunnels under the Mersey were built, huge swathes of houses were demolished and people moved away, causing the church's decline. Nearby are the ruins of Birkenhead Priory, founded by the Benedictines in 1150 and now an Exhibition Centre.

Between St Mary's Church and the Priory lies the grave of John Laird and other members of the Laird family. John Laird had joined his father's ironworks firm in 1828 and it became William Laird & Son. It was John who built up the town and developed the shipbuilding empire into a world-famous name.

The Changing Face of Merseyside

Cammell Laird was one of the biggest employers on the Wirral. Their world-famous yard turned out some of the biggest ships ever to float, and produced many famous warships such as Ark Royal, Prince of Wales and Achilles. After the war, as well as orders for liners, tankers and cross-Channel ferries, they built submarines for the Royal Navy. This is the launching of HMS *Revenge* in March 1968.

The Queen Mother came to Cammell Laird on 23 June 1959 to launch RMS *Windsor Castle* for the Union Castle line.

BIRKENHEAD

One of the more unusual attractions on the Wirral is the Historic Warships Collection at Birkenhead. Star of the show has to be the U-boat U 534, seen here on display in 2001. The U-boat was sunk in May 1945 and raised from the Kattegat, a sea passage between Jutland and Sweden, in 1993. It arrived in Birkenhead in 1996 and is the only U-boat in preservation in Great Britain. It is an awesome sight and still evokes strong feelings in many old merchant seamen who lost comrades and relatives on ships sunk by this submarine. The collection also contains the Falklands veterans HMS *Plymouth* and the HMS *Onyx*.

Ellesmere Port

The Shell Oil Refinery at Ellesmere Port, pictured c.1960.

An early 1960s view of Whitby Road, Ellesmere Port. The town was named after Lord Ellesmere, who took over the Bridgewater Estates after the death of the 3rd Duke.

New Brighton

The Tower, New Brighton, built in the late 1890s by a consortium of businessmen who wanted it to rival Blackpool Tower. At its base was a splendid theatre and ballroom, surrounded by lovely ornamental gardens. It was a huge attraction up to World War One, during which it suffered neglect. It was closed for safety reasons in 1919 and by 1921 the tower itself had gone, leaving only the tower buildings and ballroom.

Victoria Road, New Brighton, leading down to the pier, probably around 1904. This view was used on postcards printed in Germany but sold locally.

New Brighton beach at the turn of the 19th century. New Brighton was the 'Queen' of the Wirral's resorts and even rivalled Blackpool.

New Brighton

One of the glories of New Brighton was the large open-air bathing pool which could accommodate 3,000 bathers, while there was room for 30,000 spectators. These people are watching a Miss New Brighton Bathing Beauty competition just before the start of World War Two.

New Brighton

Arriving at New Brighton, crowds were met by trams to take them on to other resorts although most would stay here. This view dates from around 1912.

Built in 1934, New Brighton's bathing pool was for many years it was one of the largest and best-appointed open-air pools in the world. On this picture the pool is quiet but some of the shops can be seen. Patrons could buy anything from a bathing costume to a bag of fish and chips.

The pier at New Brighton was really two piers side-by-side. The nearest one on this picture was the ferry pier and floated up and down with the tide. The other, which was fixed, was the promenade pier.

Crowds queuing to leave the ferry at New Brighton in the late 1950s. (*Keith G. Medley*)

New Brighton

New Brighton Fun Fair in the late 1950s. its age and waning popularity beginning to show. Across the river can be seen the docks and warehouses that lined the river in those days before the decline in cargo shipping hit Liverpool. (*F. Leonard Jackson*)

Port Sunlight

The monument at Port Sunlight erected by the citizens in memory of William Hesketh Lever, first Viscount Leverhulme. He was born in Bolton in 1851, the son of a grocer. By the mid-1880s he had begun to specialise in the manufacture of soap. He always strived to make his soap product that bit better than everyone else's, making it from vegetable oils rather than tallow, and giving it a pleasant scent and neatly wrapping each bar. He built Port Sunlight out of his dreams, and took workers from the slums of Liverpool, Warrington and Manchester and gave them a dream home in a garden city, surely one of his greatest achievements. One of his sayings was: "There is nothing ugly, there is a good side to everything.". When he was asked to accept a title, William Lever decided to add his wife's maiden name, Hulme, to keep her memory alive, and he became Lord Leverhulme. His business continued to grow long after he died, becoming one of the largest concerns of its kind in the world. Today, Port Sunlight is still a charming and beautiful place to live or to visit, an oasis of peace and tranquillity.

The Lady Lever Art Gallery & Museum, Port Sunlight, seen today. When William Lever's wife died, he decided to build a magnificent edifice in her honour. He took all the treasures from his own home and filled what is, even today, one of the greatest art galleries in the country. The foundation stone was laid by King George V in 1914 and the building was opened by Princess Beatrice in December 1922.

Port Sunlight

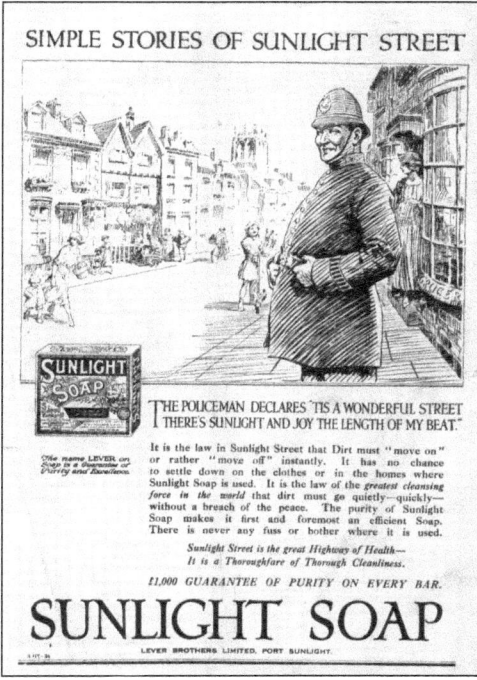

An advertisement for Sunlight Soap from a 1922 edition of the *Family Herald*, 'a domestic magazine of useful information and amusement'.

Residents of Port Sunlight enjoying their surrounding in the summer of 2001.

Lord Leverhulme was a great philanthropist. This is the men's club – it served no alcohol – which he built for his workers. The bridge is a reminder of all the channels and small rivers that once ran through the area.

Port Sunlight

The Bridge Inn at Port Sunlight as it looks in 2002. John Hesketh believed that a man should have the right to drink and so allowed a pub to be built in his village.

Wallasey

The New Promenade at Wallasey in the early 1920s. Although not as commercialised as some of the other resorts on the Wirral, Wallasey was very popular with those who wanted a quieter holiday.

This building off Bayswater Road, Wallasey, overlooking Liverpool Bay, was once the Derby Baths. It is at the start of a coastal walk and cycle track known as the North Wirral Coast Park along the Wallasey Embankment. Today it has been turned into a very popular restaurant, and leisure complex.

Southport

Quieter than its neighbour Blackpool further up the Lancashire coast, Southport has always had a reputation for elegance and quality. Formerly known as South Hawes, it got its name when Lytham was the north port on the River Ribble and the port south of the river became... Southport. Southport is now part of the Merseyside 'county'.

An Edwardian view of Lord Street, Southport, and some of its elegant shops.

Lord Street, Southport, in the 1920s. The tall building on the right is the Scarisbrick Hotel, still there and busy as ever today. Note the two trams, one a single-deck, and how far over the power poles had to come.

The Changing Face of Merseyside

Shoppers on Lord Street looking for gifts for Christmas on a cold December day in 1931.

Southport

Looking down on Lord Street c.1908. The long the gardens on the houses and hotels on the right of the street have been cut back today to widen Lord Street. The first tower (centre of picture) is Southport Town Hall, and the other two are of churches.

Lord Street, Southport, frozen in time in August 1971. A Southport Corporation bus heads for Westcliffe Road, on route 19. (*J. A. Sommerfield*)

SOUTHPORT

The Gardens in Lord Street and the Grand Cinema behind, c.1956.

The Promenade, Southport, c.1956. Compared with the photograph on the next page, the road is much wider now but the gardens are still more or less the same.

The Promenade, Southport. Note the horse-drawn coaches full of trippers and the large gardens in front of the guest houses and hotels along the Promenade. The picture is probably from around the time of World War One.

Southport

The Changing Face of Merseyside

SOUTHPORT

There are a lot of unkind jokes about how far out the tide goes out at Southport, but in this picture from c.1927 the visitors all seem to be enjoying themselves.

One of Southport's many attractions is the Miniature Railway, started by D. Ladmore, a local dentist. This picture is from 1918 when Pleasure Land was called White City, as the station sign shows.

Another view of the Miniature Railway terminus, this time in 1950. The steam engine here looks like the one which came from Rhyl Marine Railway when it closed in 1948. Note the famous three bridges across the lake behind.

Chapel Street railway station in June 1951. Southport's main station is pictured here when steam trains still ruled. (*J.A. Peden*)

Widnes

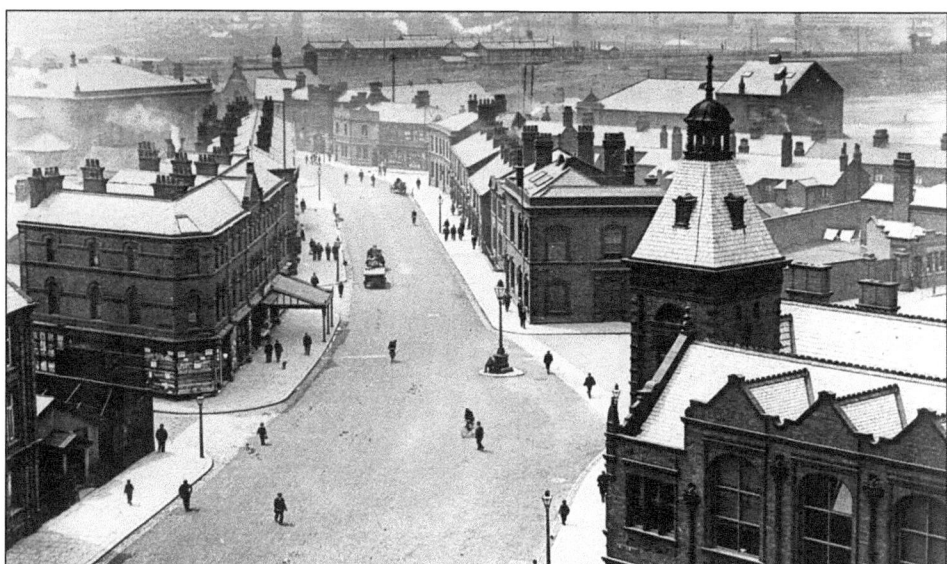

Looking from the top of St Paul's Church, Victoria Square, Widnes, c.1906. Boot's Cash Chemist is on the left with a hotel next to it. The Victoria Road Methodist Church (now the Queen's Hall) is the square building behind them. The tower to the right is the Technical School and Library with the Magistrates Court just behind. The tall building to the top right of the picture is the Alexandra Theatre. The Police Station is next to the Magistrates Court and the light-coloured building in the very centre of the street is the Sun Inn.

Victoria Square, dominated by St Paul's Church and the Technical School, seen here in the 1950s.

WIDNES

Victoria Road Methodist Church at the beginning of the 20th century.

Albert Road, Widnes, c.1900. The open space on the right became the Premier cinema, and the house on the right belonged to 'Bozza' Martin. Bozza, who lived in Appleton Village, had it pulled down and built a cinema called Bozzadrom. It later became the Regal.

The Changing Face of Merseyside

Local people in procession to the opening of the War Memorial in Victoria Park in the early 1920s.

Hough Green corner looking from Hough Green Station. Liverpool Road runs across the back of the photograph and the houses in the middle of the picture are on Ditchfield Road corner.

WIDNES

The thatched cottage which once stood on Farnworth Street. This view looks down from the church. Today, Russell Court can be seen from this point.

Widnes players tour the town after their losing RL Challenge Cup Final at Wembley in 1934. They went down 11-5 to Hunslet.

The Changing Face of Merseyside

Naughton Park, home of Widnes RLFC, in the early 1960s. Under these primitive floodlights, the Chemics won the BBC2 Floodlit Trophy on more than one occasion.

Two Widnes Corporation buses wait for passengers to come off the Transporter Car in 1950. The bus nearest the camera had in front of it a one-hour journey to Rainhill. (*Abcross*)

WIDNES

The scene at West Bank Dock about a century ago. Widnes, Runcorn and the Mersey had their own unique sailing vessels, some of which are pictured here.

West Bank, Widnes, c.1900, just before work started on the Transporter Bridge. Right of the picture are some of the chemical factories which lined the St Helens Canal.

The tower of the Transporter Bridge on the Runcorn side during construction. The towers were 90ft high and the distance across was 333 yards, which took cars an average of four minutes to cross. if necessary cars would give way to traffic on the Manchester Ship Canal.

WIDNES

The Widnes-Runcorn Railway Bridge, as it was officially called, opened in July 1861 by the London & North-Western Railway Company. Runcorn Church can be seen through the arches.

The Transporter Bridge pictured c.1910.

Runcorn

A view from Runcorn's Market Square looking south towards the Magistrates Court, c.1908. Runcorn Baths is just off camera on the right. Note the stalls of the original Runcorn Market.

Highlands Road, Higher Runcorn, pictured over a century ago.

Runcorn

Waterloo Road, Runcorn, looking down towards the entrance to the Transporter Bridge in the late 19th century. The road was laid out not long after the Battle of Waterloo in 1815, and named after it. In years to come the road would be clogged with traffic waiting its turn at the bridge. In summer, at weekends, the wait could be as long as two hours, forcing some motorists to head off to Warrington to cross the Mersey at Bridgefoot.

A Crosville double-decker bus, 12A, waiting for the next Transport car, to take passengers to Helsby via Rocksavage and Frodsham. The turning circle was on the left of the picture, outside the Waterloo Inn.

Timber ships at Saltport, below Runcorn, on 22 July 1892. The water was admitted up to Weston Marsh Lock from 28 September 1891.